GO EAT PIZZA

A BUFFET OF PIZZA HISTORY, RECIPES, AND FUN

GLUTEN-FREE & DAIRY-FREE OPTIONS

GAIL M. NELSON

piz·za *noun*
A baked pie of Italian origin consisting of a shallow breadlike crust covered with seasoned sauce, cheese, and other toppings.

Go Eat Pizza is written and illustrated by Gail M. Nelson.

Copyright © 2011, Gail M. Nelson; Ready Set Go Eat LLC

2nd Edition © 2013, Gail M. Nelson

Ready, Set, Go Eat books, games, etc. are available at bulk discounts for educational use, fund-raisers, or sales promotions. The author is available for presentations and signing books.

Please contact Gail at GailNelson421@gmail.com for more information or visit GailMNelson.com.

This book is dedicated to all kids–and dogs–who love pizza. ~ GN

Thank you to Angelica, Hannah, Katie, Andrew, Madison, and Samantha for participating in Pizza Camp.

NOTE: Cooking and other activities in this book require active adult supervision to ensure children's safety and fun. Join in the project with them and be sure they know what they are doing before they try it alone.

The publisher and author assume no responsibility for injuries or damage while performing any activities in this book, nor for the results.

INTRODUCTION

What is a dog's favorite pizza?

¡Pepperoni!

Put your nose into this pizza lover's book. Paw through over thirty fun and easy recipes for homemade pizza. You can chow down on pizza five times a day!

Dig into the history of pizza. Throw a make-your-own-pizza party. Fetch fresh herbs and vegetables to bake with. Play with lots of awesome activities.

Let's sniff out more about pizza!

- *Pete*

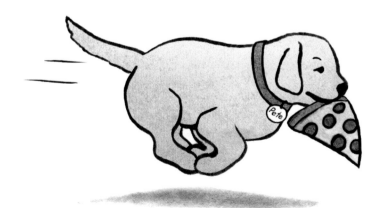

Pizza's Past

The Bread Crust

Over 2,000 years ago, in the small towns of Italy, peasants baked their bread in a community oven. Bread takes a long time to bake, so one day a baker listened to her rumbling stomach and flattened a small piece of dough to cook quickly for a snack. This snack caught on and bakers began making edible "plates" to soak up drippings and seasonings from meals.

Pizza for Breakfast

About 1,000 years ago, an early version of pizza was a favorite dish in the Roman Empire. Bakers topped discs of dough with herbs and olives, garlic and leeks, fruits and nuts, and even leftover fish. The bread was then cooked in scorching hot ovens and eaten for breakfast.

THE TOMATO

About 200 years ago, the Conquistadors of Spain brought home an exotic plant from Mexico. Europeans grew this beauty for decoration because they thought the bright red fruit was poisonous. When they discovered the tomato's wonderful flavor, it became a favorite ingredient in pizza.

THE CHEESE

King Umberto and Queen Margherita were visiting Naples, Italy in 1889. The King requested a special meal from the famous pizza chef, Raffaele Esposito, in honor of the Queen's birthday. The red, white and green of the Italian flag gave Mr. Esposito an idea. For the first time, he added Mozzarella cheese to his famous tomato and fresh basil pizza. The Queen chose it as her favorite pizza of the meal. To this day, we enjoy Margherita Pizza. The recipe can be found on page 19.

What do you call 1000 pizzas on top of each other?

The leaning tower of pizza!

Pizza in America

When Gennaro Lombardini moved to America in the late 1800's, there was no place to buy pizza. He had come from Naples, Italy, where workers and tourists could order a fresh, hot pizza folded in half and served in a piece of newspaper. These *libretti*, or little books, were readily available for take-out. In 1895, Mr. Lombardini opened America's first fast-food restaurant, a pizzeria in New York City's Little Italy.

The Pizza Business

Pizza's popularity in America increased greatly after World War II when soldiers arrived home with an appetite for fresh, hot pizza like they had eaten in Italy. The demand for pizza has continued to grow into an estimated six-billion-dollar industry in the United States today.

PIZZA IN A CONE

In 2004, Rossano Boscolo invented a stroll-and-eat pizza in the shape of an ice cream cone. It's called the Konopizza and it has a crisp crust filled with cheese, tomatoes, and many choices of toppings. This fast-food pizza bakes in just 3 minutes in a specially designed oven.

COOKING TIPS

1   Read the recipe and make sure you have everything you will need.

2   Tie back long hair.

3   Wash hands thoroughly with soap and warm water.

4   Check with an adult before using sharp knives.

5   BE VERY CAREFUL around a hot oven. Always use oven mitts with hot pans.

6   Turn on the oven 10 minutes before you'll need it. Turn off the oven when your pizza is done.

7   Clean as you go and the final clean-up will be easy.

8   Have FUN!

 Very Easy Recipe

 Easy Recipe

 More Difficult Recipe

 Ask an adult for help when you see this symbol!

PETE'S SAFETY POINTERS

▷ Taste with a clean spoon, not your paws.

▷ Wash all fruits and veggies to remove dirt and chemicals.

▷ Always cut away from yourself on a cutting board.

▷ Always use oven mitts or pot holders, never a wet towel.

▷ Be careful not to burn your tail. If you do get a burn, hold it under cold running water, then apply aloe vera.

Pre-made, gluten-free crusts and dairy-free cheese substitutes are becoming easier to find. The Gluten-free Cornmeal Crust (page 35) can be substituted for any crust in the reipes. A tasty dairy-free cheese is Daiya brand Mozzarella style shreds.

BREAKFAST PIZZA

Crust
1 whole grain English muffin (gluten-free, if desired)

Toppings
strawberry or raspberry jam
1 oz. string cheese (or Daiya Mozzarella Style Shreds)
1 small box raisins

1 On a plate, slice string cheese into circles with a butter knife.

2 Spread jam on top of each half of an English muffin.

3 Sprinkle with cheese and raisins.

4 Bake two to three minutes at 350° in a toaster oven or cover with an upside down bowl and microwave 30 seconds to melt the cheese. Remove carefully with a pot holder.

Serves one.

Do you feel
like a pizza?

No, do I
look like one?

FRENCH TOAST PIZZA

Crust
1 slice frozen or pre-cooked French toast
(gluten-free, if desired)

Toppings
1 oz. cottage cheese (or Daiya Mozzarella Style Shreds)
maple syrup
assorted berries, fresh or frozen

1 Wash berries. Thaw if needed.

2 Scoop a large spoonful of cottage cheese into a
bowl. Sweeten with a little maple syrup.

3 Heat french toast in a toaster or
toaster oven. Carefully place on
a plate.

4 Spread cottage cheese mixture on top
of hot French toast.

5 Top with your favorite berries.

Serves one.

Dr. Suess Pizza

Crust
3 eggs
3 drops green food coloring
½ teaspoon olive oil

Toppings
2 oz. Mozzarella cheese, shredded
(or Daiya Mozzarella Style Shreds)
⅛ cup ham, cubed
tomato, onion, etc., chopped

1 Prepare the toppings.

2 Break eggs into a bowl and beat lightly with a fork. Add food coloring to eggs and stir well.

3 Heat oil in a frying pan over medium-low heat. Slowly pour in egg mixture.

4 Cover and cook until eggs are set, about 2 to 5 minutes. Do not stir! (Jiggle the pan lightly to see if eggs are cooked through.)

5 Turn heat down to low. Flip eggs and top with cheese and ham. Add other toppings, if desired.

6 Cover and cook 2 minutes more. Slice into wedges.

Serves two.

ITALIAN PIZZA

Crust
Foccacia bread or Flatbread (gluten-free, if desired)

Toppings
Italian Sauce or Easy White Sauce (page 31)
oregano (fresh or dried)
basil (fresh or dried)
tomato, chopped and drained on a paper towel
4 oz. Mozzarella cheese, grated
(or Daiya Mozzarella Style Shreds)

1 Slice, dice and prepare the toppings.

2 Heat oven to 450° F. Place the foccacia or flat bread on a baking sheet.

3 Spoon sauce on top and spread out evenly.

4 Sprinkle with herbs, tomato, and cheese.

5 Bake for 8 to 10 minutes. Remove from oven with oven mitts. Cool a couple of minutes before cutting.

Serves four.

When do astronauts eat pizza?

At launch time!

PITA PIZZA

Crust
one whole grain pita bread (gluten-free, if desired)
olive oil

Toppings
pizza or spaghetti sauce
1 oz. feta cheese, crumbled
black olives, sliced
tomato, chopped and drained on a paper towel
basil & oregano (fresh or dried)
fresh garlic or garlic powder

1 Slice, dice and prepare the toppings.

2 Heat oven to 400° F. Place pita bread on a baking sheet and brush a little olive oil on top. Bake in the oven for 2 to 4 minutes. Remove baking sheet with oven mitts.

3 Spoon a little pizza or spaghetti sauce on pita.

4 Top with cheese, olives, tomatoes, herbs and a sprinkle of garlic.

5 Bake for 7 to 8 minutes more, or until pita is crispy. Remove from oven with oven mitts. Cool a couple of minutes before cutting into wedges.

Serves one.

PESTO SANDWICH PIZZA

Crust
2 slices of bread or 1 sandwich roll,
(gluten-free, if desired)

Toppings
1 tablespoon pesto sauce (page 30)
1 oz. Mozzarella cheese, grated
¼ cup pepperoni or artichoke quarters, diced
1 small tomato, chopped and drained on a paper towel

1 Spoon pesto sauce onto bread and spread evenly with back of spoon.

2 Mix cheese, pepperoni or artichokes, and tomato together in a bowl. Place mixture on top of pesto. Cover with a slice of bread or top of roll. Wrap in aluminum foil.

3 Heat in a toaster oven or regular oven at 350° F. until cheese has melted and outside is toasty, about 10-15 minutes.

Serves one.

Where
does a spider
order a pizza?

On the web!

EASY VEGGIE PIZZA

Crust
one whole wheat or corn tortilla

Toppings
olive oil
ranch-style dressing
black olives, sliced
peppers & onions, diced
fresh mushrooms, sliced
2 oz. cheddar jack cheese, shredded
(or Daiya PepperJack Style Shreds)

1 Place tortilla on a baking sheet and brush lightly with olive oil.

2 Preheat toaster oven or oven to 400° F. Bake for 2 minutes. Remove with oven mitts.

3 Spoon a little ranch dressing on the tortilla and spread evenly.

4 Top with olives, peppers, mushrooms, onions and cheese.

5 Bake for 2 to 3 minutes more or until cheese has melted. Remove from oven with oven mitts. Cool a few minutes before cutting into wedges.

Serves one or two.

MINI PIZZA CRISPS

Crust
4 frozen rolls (dough) or gluten-free bread slices

Toppings
olive oil
4 oz. Mozzarella cheese, shredded
(or Daiya Mozzarella Style Shreds)
garlic clove, minced
basil (fresh or dried)
tomato, chopped
olives, sliced

1 Thaw rolls as directed on package. On a floured surface, flatten each roll with a rolling pin. Try tossing it in the air, if you like!

2 Brush dough circles or bread slices lightly with olive oil.

3 Sprinkle with cheese, garlic, basil, olives, and tomato, to taste.

4 Heat oven to 450° F. Put pizzas on a baking sheet and carefully place in oven. Bake 7 to 10 minutes, until golden brown and crispy. Remove with oven mitts and let cool a few minutes.

Serves two to four.

PIZZA PILLOWS

Crust
one tube refrigerated buttermilk biscuits
vegetable spray

Toppings
5 oz. shredded Mozzarella or cheddar cheese
deli meat or pepperoni
basil (fresh or dried)
garlic powder

1 Lightly grease baking sheet with non-stick vegetable spray. Preheat oven to 400° F.

2 Measure ¾ cup shredded cheese into a bowl.

3 Chop ½ cup deli meat or pepperoni. Add to cheese. Stir in spices, to taste.

4 Open biscuit can and press 5 biscuits flat on baking sheet. Put one spoonful of filling in the center of each biscuit. Flatten remaining biscuits and place over filling. Press edges of dough together all the way around each pair of biscuits with a fork.

5 Bake 10 to 12 minutes, until golden brown. Remove pan with oven mitts and let cool a few minutes before eating.

Makes five pillows.

MARGHERITA PIZZA

Crust
Traditional Crust (see page 32)

Toppings
¼ cup No-Cook Tomato Sauce (page 28) or spaghetti sauce
6 fresh basil leaves
6 oz. Mozzarella cheese, thinly sliced

1 Prepare pizza dough on a round pan. Preheat oven to 425° F.

2 Spread tomato or spaghetti sauce evenly on top of the pizza dough.

3 Top with basil leaves and Mozzarella slices.

4 Bake until edges are golden brown and cheese is melted, about 12 to 15 minutes. Slice and enjoy a royal meal.

Serves four.

For the story of Queen Margherita's pizza see page 5.

PETE-ZA

Crust
one tube refrigerated pizza dough or
Multi-grain Crust Recipe (see page 33)

Toppings
1 tablespoon olive oil
6 oz. shredded Mozzarella cheese
(or Daiya Mozzarella Style Shreds)
Sun-Dried Tomato Sauce (page 29) or spaghetti sauce
2 slices pepperoni
1 bunch chives
2 black olives

1 Grease pizza pan or baking sheet with olive oil. Preheat oven.

2 Sprinkle work surface and dough lightly with flour. Shape the dough into three balls, one large ball for the face and two small balls for the ears. Roll out the large ball with a rolling pin into a 10- to 12-inch circle. Place the flattened dough on an oiled pan. Shape the small balls into ears, as shown, overlapping the face. Brush dough with oil.

What does an aardvark like on a pizza?

Ant-chovies!

3 Spread a little sauce on the ears and under the chin.

4 Sprinkle face with shredded cheese.

5 Make nose and tongue with pepperoni. Make whiskers and eyebrows with chives and eyes with black olives.

6 Bake according to directions for desired crust.

Serves four.

NACHO PIZZA

Crust
one tube of refrigerated crescent roll dough
or Gluten-free Cornmeal Crust (page 35)

Toppings
Spicy Tomato Sauce (page 29)
½ lb. ground beef or 2 veggie burgers
1 tablespoon taco seasoning
½ cup sour cream or plain yogurt
1 8 oz. bag tortilla chips, crushed
6 oz. cheddar jack or pepper jack cheese, grated
(or Daiya PepperJack Style Shreds)
cherry tomatoes and/or salsa

1 Brown ground beef in a frying pan and drain grease. Or chop thawed veggie burgers into small pieces. Sprinkle with taco seasoning and stir well.

2 Spray pizza pan or baking sheet with non-stick baking spray. Open crescent roll dough or make Cornmeal Crust and press onto pan. Heat oven to 350° F. for crescent rolls or 425° F. for Cornmeal Crust.

3 Place toppings on crust, in order: sauce, ½ bag crushed chips, seasoned ground beef or veggie burger, sour cream or yogurt, and shredded cheese. Add remaining chips.

4 Bake for 20 to 25 minutes, until crust is golden brown. Remove from oven and cool 5 minutes. Top with tomatoes and salsa, if desired.

Serves four.

MAMA MIA'S PESTO PIZZA

Crust
Multi-grain Crust (page 33)

Toppings
Pesto sauce (page 30)
6 oz. Mozzarella cheese, shredded
(or Daiya Mozzarella Style Shreds)
½ cup black olives, pitted & sliced
½ cup fresh mushrooms, sliced
1 red bell pepper, diced
1 tomato, chopped
spinach leaves, chopped

1 Prepare pizza dough according to directions. Preheat oven to 475° F.

2 Spread 2 tablespoons of pesto evenly over the dough with the back of a spoon. (Use the leftover pesto on noodles or freeze for another meal.)

3 Add your favorite toppings and sprinkle with Mozzarella cheese.

4 Bake 12 to 15 minutes, until top and crust are golden brown. Cool a few minutes and cut into wedges. Serve with grated parmesan cheese, if desired.

5 For dessert, save your crust edges and top with honey.

Serves four.

POTATO PIZZA

Crust
Gluten-free Cornmeal Crust (page 35)

Toppings
1 lb. potatoes
2 tablespoons olive oil
1 tablespoon fresh rosemary leaves
1 teaspoon black pepper, freshly ground

1 Prepare Cornmeal Crust as directed, varying the shape, if desired. Preheat oven to 450° F.

2 Scrub potatoes well and pat dry. Slice as thinly as possible.

3 Brush dough with a little olive oil, then arrange the potatoes on top. Sprinkle with rosemary and pepper. Drizzle remaining olive oil over the top.

4 Bake for 25 minutes, until crust is golden brown and crisp underneath.

Serves 4.

GREEK PIZZA

Crust
½ lb. phyllo dough, thawed

Toppings
6 tablespoons olive oil
½ cup bread crumbs
2 large, ripe plum tomatoes
1 red, yellow, or orange bell pepper, or 5 pepperoncinis,
sliced thinly
2 garlic cloves, minced
3 green onions, sliced
1 cup pitted, sliced Kalamata olives
4 oz. feta or goat cheese
4 oz. shredded Mozzarella cheese
Dried oregano and freshly ground black pepper, to taste

1 Preheat oven to 450° F. Prepare a sheet of plastic wrap to cover dough while working.

2 Lightly brush a large rectangular baking sheet with oil. Layer 8 to 10 sheets of phyllo dough evenly on the pan, brushing each layer with olive oil.

3 Spread bread crumbs on a shallow dish and dredge tomatoes lightly to absorb juice. Place on crust.

4 Layer with pepper slices, garlic, onions, and olives. Top with cheese and sprinkle with oregano and black pepper.

5 Bake 12 to 20 minutes, until cheese is melted and edges are golden brown and crispy.

Serves 4.

FRUIT BLAST PIZZA

Crust
1 tube refrigerated sugar cookie dough

Toppings
fresh fruit: berries, kiwi, bananas, etc.
8 oz. cream cheese, softened
2 tablespoons brown sugar
1 teaspoon vanilla

1 Heat oven to 350° F. Spray pizza pan with non-stick spray. Press cookie dough flat on the pan by hand.

2 Bake 12 to 15 minutes in preheated oven. Remove crust from oven with oven mitts. Cool completely.

3 Wash fruit in large strainer. Cut into bite-size pieces.

4 Beat cream cheese, brown sugar and vanilla together.

5 Spread the cream cheese mixture on top of the cool crust with a rubber spatula. Place fruit all over the top. Cut into wedges.

Makes one 12" pizza. Individual cookie pizzas are fun, too!

STRAWBERRY SHORTCAKE PIZZA

Crust
2 cups flour
8 oz. plain yogurt
1 tablespoon
baking powder
1 egg
¼ cup vegetable oil

Toppings
2 pints fresh strawberries
8 oz. Cool Whip® or whipped cream

1 Wash strawberries in a strainer; remove stems. Cut berries in half and set aside.

2 Mix flour, yogurt, baking powder, egg and vegetable oil. Knead on a floured board for 2 or 3 minutes, adding more flour if sticky, until dough is smooth and elastic.

3 Roll out dough in a circle a little larger than the pizza pan. Sprinkle pan with flour and slip dough onto the pan. Roll up edges of the dough to make a rim. Place a pie plate on top of the dough to keep it from bubbling up while cooking.

4 Bake 15 minutes at 450° F. Take crust out of the oven and remove the pie plate. Cool crust completely before continuing.

5 Spread Cool Whip® or whipped cream over the crust with a rubber spatula. Place strawberries on top, cut side down. To serve, slice into wedges with a pizza wheel.

Makes one 12" pizza.

No-Cook Tomato Sauce

Ingredients

1 6-oz. can tomato paste
1 16-oz. can whole tomatoes, drained & cut up with spoon
2 cloves garlic, minced, or ¼ teaspoon garlic powder
1 teaspoon oregano
1 teaspoon basil
1 teaspoon olive oil
¼ cup minced onion or 1 teaspoon onion flakes

1 In a large bowl, mix all ingredients together well.

2 Spoon sauce on top of an unbaked pizza crust. Add toppings.

3 Bake as directed for the crust recipe.

NOTE: Leftover sauce is tasty on pasta, too!

Knock, knock.
Who's there?
Pasta. Pasta who?
Pasta pizza, please.

SUN-DRIED TOMATO SAUCE

Ingredients

1 small jar sun-dried tomatoes in olive oil
1 tablespoon chopped, fresh basil
No-Cook Tomato Sauce (page 28)

1 Drain and purée sun-dried tomatoes. Add the purée and finely chopped basil leaves to the No-Cook Tomato Sauce. Mix well.

SPICY TOMATO SAUCE

Ingredients

1 or 2 fresh red or green chili peppers
No-Cook Tomato Sauce (page 28)

1 Finely chop spicy chilies, to taste. Add to the No-Cook Tomato Sauce.

PESTO SAUCE

Ingredients
1 large bunch fresh basil (about 2 cups of leaves)
1 small bunch fresh parsley (about 1 cup of leaves)
¾ cup pine nuts
2 cloves garlic, pressed
6 tablespoons olive oil
1 cup fresh parmesan cheese, grated (optional)

1 Place basil, parsley, pine nuts, garlic and olive oil in a blender or food processor. Blend well. Turn on and off, scraping sides often with a rubber spatula.

2 Place pesto mixture in a bowl and stir in the parmesan cheese.

3 To store pesto, freeze in an ice cube tray. One or two cubes are the right amount for one pizza. After pesto is frozen solid, pop out the cubes and place in a freezer bag or plastic container. Remove cubes from the freezer to thaw about an hour before you are ready to make pizza.

NOTE: Leftover sauce is tasty on pasta, too!

Easy White Sauce

Ingredients

½ cup ranch-style dressing
1 large garlic clove, minced
Dash of Italian seasoning

1 In a small bowl, mix all ingredients together with a spoon.

2 Spoon sauce on top of an unbaked pizza crust. Add toppings.

3 Bake as directed for the crust recipe.

Easy Italian Sauce

Ingredients

½ cup italian-style dressing
1 large garlic clove, minced

1 In a small bowl, mix ingredients together with a spoon.

2 Spoon sauce on top of an unbaked pizza crust. Add toppings.

3 Bake as directed for the crust recipe.

TRADITIONAL CRUST

Ingredients

2 cups all-purpose flour
1 teaspoon salt
2¼ teaspoons rapid-rise yeast
2 tablespoons olive oil
1 cup very warm water (not hot!)

1 Mix flour and salt in a large mixing bowl. Add yeast, olive oil and water. Mix together with a spoon or fingers. Sprinkle some extra flour on the counter and knead the dough by folding, flattening and turning for 5 minutes, until smooth.

2 Oil a clean bowl, place dough inside and cover it. Leave in a warm place for one hour, until the dough has risen to double its size.

3 When ready, sprinkle work surface with flour. Form dough into a ball and sprinkle with flour. Roll it out with a rolling pin, turning the dough often. Sprinkle with more flour if it gets sticky. Roll into a 12- to 14-inch circle.

4 Place dough on an oiled pan. Pinch edges up to form a crust. Add favorite toppings. Bake in a preheated oven at 425° for 12 to 15 minutes.

MULTI-GRAIN CRUST

Ingredients

½ cup very warm water (not hot!)
1⅛ teaspoon rapid-rise yeast
½ tablespoon honey
½ tablespoon olive oil
¾ cup all-purpose (or gluten-free) flour
¼ cup whole wheat (or gluten-free) flour
¼ cup oat flour
⅛ cup sesame seeds

1 Dissolve yeast and honey in water. Add olive oil and flour. Combine into a sticky, gooey mess. Turn out onto a floured surface and knead the dough by folding, flattening and turning for 5 minutes, until smooth. Place dough in an oiled bowl. Cover and let stand until double in size (about 30 to 40 minutes.)

2 Sprinkle counter with a little flour. Form dough into a ball and sprinkle with flour. Roll out with a rolling pin, turning the dough often. Sprinkle with more flour as needed. Form a 12- to 14-inch circle and place on an oiled pan. Pinch edges up for the crust.

3 Add favorite toppings. Bake in a preheated oven at 425°, 12 to 15 minutes.

What do pizza chefs depend on the most?

They knead the dough!

WHOLE WHEAT CRUST

Ingredients

1½ cups whole wheat flour
1 tablespoon baking powder
½ teaspoon salt
½ cup plus 2 tablespoons warm water
2 tablespoons olive oil

1 Mix flour, baking powder, and salt in a large mixing bowl. Make a well in the center and add olive oil and water. Mix together with a spoon or fingers.

2 Sprinkle some extra flour on the counter and knead the dough by folding, flattening and turning for 5 minutes, until smooth. After kneading, it is ready to roll out.

3 Sprinkle work surface with flour. Form dough into a ball and sprinkle with flour. Roll it out with a rolling pin, turning the dough often. Sprinkle with more flour if it gets sticky. Roll into a 12- to 14-inch circle.

4 Place dough on an oiled pan. Pinch edges up to form a crust. Add favorite toppings. Bake in a preheated oven at 425° for 12 to 15 minutes.

GLUTEN-FREE CORNMEAL CRUST

Ingredients

½ cup gluten-free cornmeal
1 cup gluten-free flour
2 teaspoons baking powder
½ teaspoon salt
½ cup warm water
2 tablespoons olive oil

1 Mix cornmeal, gluten-free flour, baking powder, and salt in a large mixing bowl. Make a well in the center and add olive oil and water. Mix together with a spoon or fingers.

2 Sprinkle some extra flour on the counter and knead the dough by folding, flattening and turning for 5 minutes, until smooth. After kneading, it is ready to use.

3 Place dough on an oiled pan. Form dough into a ball and sprinkle with flour. Press out the dough with fingertips, from the center to the outside edge. Make an 11- to 12-inch circle. Sprinkle with more flour if it gets sticky. Pinch edges up to form a crust. Add favorite toppings.

4 Bake in a preheated oven at 425° for 10 to 15 minutes.

PIZZA CREATURES

Create critters out of pizza dough and toppings. Bake until light brown and crispy, about 8 to 12 minutes. Cool and play with your food!

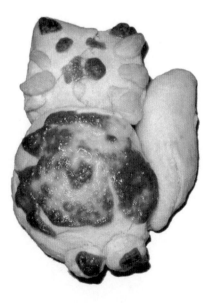

KOOL-AID®
CLAY PIZZA

Ingredients
1 cup flour
1 tablespoon vegetable oil
1 pkg. unsweetened Kool-Aid®
¼ cup salt
2 tablespoons cream of tartar
1 cup water

1 Mix together dry ingredients in a medium pot. Add water and oil. Stir well with wooden spoon.

2 Stir over medium heat for 3 to 5 minutes. Keep stirring the whole time! When mixture forms a ball in the pot, remove from pan. Let clay cool.

3 Knead clay by folding, flattening and turning until it is smooth.

4 Make 3 or 4 batches with various flavors of Kool-Aid®.

5 Roll out one color of clay with the rolling pin for a pizza crust. Make toppings out of different colors of clay. Experiment with mixing colors to get brown, orange, etc. Create a unique Kool-Aid® Clay pizza.

Note: Clay is edible, but tastes yucky!

To play another day, store leftover clay in plastic bags in the refrigerator.

PIZZA PARTY WITH PIZZAZZ

GET READY TO PARTY

▷ Chop favorite toppings for do-it-yourself pizzas and store in the refrigerator before the party starts.

▷ Cover a table with white paper and provide crayons or markers for games and drawing.

▷ Set table with fun plates, cups and napkins.

▷ Make the pizza dough.

▷ Prepare the sauce.

▷ Start the music!

HOLIDAY PIZZAS

Fun crust shapes to try:

Balloon ~ Birthday

Heart ~ Valentine's Day

Shamrock ~ St. Patrick's Day

Star ~ Independence Day

Pumpkin ~ Halloween

PIZZA
TOPPING
SMORGASBORD

Pizza Sauce

Olives

Peppers

Onions

Tomatoes

Fresh Basil

Garlic

Shrimp

Pineapple

Ham

Jalapenos

Pepperoni

Artichoke Hearts

Spinach

Canadian Bacon

Cheese and/or
Dairy-free selection

Glossary

Utensils Needed to Make Pizza

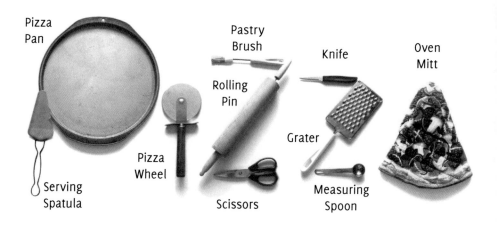

Pizza Pan

Pastry Brush

Knife

Oven Mitt

Rolling Pin

Grater

Pizza Wheel

Serving Spatula

Scissors

Measuring Spoon

Resources

The Complete Book of Pizza by Louise Love. Sassafras Press, 1980.

Cooking the Italian Way by Alphonse Bisignano. Lerner Publications, 2002.

Dinner from Dirt by Emily Scott and Catherine Duffy, Illustrated by Denise Kirby. Gibbs Smith Publisher, 1998.

I Made It Myself! by Sandra Nissenberg, R.D. and Heather Nissenberg. Sandra Nissenberg, 1998.

The Little Guide to Pizzas. Fog City Press, 2000.

Web Sites

italian.about.com

cleanjoke.com

Made in the USA
Middletown, DE
01 April 2022

63411885R00024